DIL KE ALFAAZ

WRITTEN BY KUNAL ROY

Love, Loss, and the Poetry In Between

Author Kunal Roy

WRITTEN BY KUNAL ROY

Copyright

All About You

This book is a work of emotion and imagination.
Any resemblance to actual events, persons, or locations is purely coincidental unless otherwise stated.

First Edition: August 2025
ISBN: 978-93-343-7974-7
Language: English
Author: Kunal Roy
Email: contact@kunalroy.in
Instagram: @author.kunaltoy
Website: www.medium.com/@kunalroy

Cover & Interior Design: By the Author
Publisher: Self-Published

This is a self-published digital edition.
For feedback, queries, or collaborations, please reach out via the contact details above.

Love, Loss, and the Poetry In Between

Dedication

To the one I never truly got to know... and yet somehow, always knew. This book is for the silent spaces between us the moments that were never captured in photos, the words that were never spoken out loud, and the feelings that remained tucked quietly in the corners of our hearts. You may never read this. You may not even remember the little stories we built, unintentionally, through small gestures and passing glances. But I do. Every page in this book carries the weight of unspoken emotions. laughter that never made it to conversations, goodbyes that never happened properly, and love that was real but never had a name. This is not just poetry. These are memories. Fragments. Echoes. Hopes. Goodbyes. All wrapped into words I wish I could've said. If life had offered us another version of the same story, maybe one where timing was kinder, where circumstances aligned, perhaps this would've ended differently. But maybe it was always meant to end like this: quietly, beautifully, and unfinished. So, I dedicate DIL KE ALFAAZ to the version of you that exists only in my heart.
The version who inspired love, silence, healing, and art.

Thank you,
For being unknowingly unforgettable.

With all that was left unsaid,
Kunal Roy

My smile is just a broken poem in disguise.

Acknowledgements

Writing "DIL KE ALFAAZ" has been a deeply personal journey, one that pulled pieces of my heart onto the page, sometimes with ease and sometimes with resistance.

First and foremost, I want to thank the unnamed muse behind these words. Though you may never know the depth of your presence in these verses, your silent inspiration helped shape every line, every pause, every ache within this book. This was never just about love, it was about what lingers when love fades, and what remains even when everything else disappears.

To my readers, thank you for giving your time, your heart, and your imagination to these pages. If any poem here made you pause, smile, cry, or remember someone from your past, then my purpose has been fulfilled.

To my friends and silent supporters, thank you for standing by me during the quiet phases of writing, for understanding my distance, and for encouraging me when I questioned myself.

Special gratitude to those who believe in self-expression, who know the healing power of poetry, and who understand that sometimes, we write not for answers but for peace.

Lastly, to myself for being brave enough to feel it all, and gentle enough to let it go... through poetry.

With love and sincerity,
Kunal Roy

You left...
but the silence stayed forever.

Introduction

Welcome to DIL KE ALFAAZ, a collection of emotions, memories, and moments captured in words.

This book is not just about poetry; it's about people. It's about you, the one who stayed, the one who left, the one who never knew. Every shayari in this collection is a reflection of feelings that often go unspoken love that never found words, pain that remained silent, and hope that quietly waited in the background.

While writing this book, I didn't follow rules or structures. I simply followed the heart. Each line was born from a moment that touched me deeply sometimes with joy, sometimes with heartbreak. The purpose wasn't to impress, but to express.

Through these pages, you may find your own untold stories. Perhaps a verse will remind you of someone you loved, or a moment you lost, or maybe even the version of yourself you used to be.
This book is for the lovers, the dreamers, the broken, the healed, and everyone in between. If these words touch even one soul, bring one smile, or heal one heart then it was all worth it.

Thank you for picking up DIL KE ALFAAZ. I hope you find something real within these pages something that stays with you long after the last line.

— Kunal Roy

Some goodbyes
never stop echoing.

Table of Contents

**I lost you once,
but I lose you every day in my memory.**

I'm a Poet

1.
I'm a poet, And the greatest tragedy of a poet's life is, they fall in love with beautiful girls, only to lose them to doctors or engineers.

2.
Such tragedies have happened to me many times.
It's nothing new anymore. Yet every time I lose someone I loved, a storm brews inside me. Because every relationship feels special, and every heartbreak leaves a new scar.

3.
I'm a poet. Every line I write holds meaning for someone, but that someone never reads them. She's too busy attending the wedding of an engineer.

4.
I loved her with an open heart. And she walked away with someone driving a fancy car. And I? I just kept writing poems. After all, a poet is human too... isn't he?

5.
For a poet, love means manuscripts. For a beautiful girl, love means parties, gifts, and luxury cars. And in the end, it's the poet who quietly asks,"Was that love?"

6.

I wrote a hundred poems for her, because I was a poet. And what did she do? Without reading a single line, she said "yes" to a guy with an MBA.

7.

You once asked, "What will you ever achieve by being a poet?" I smiled. Because you didn't know,
Your departure itself became the most beautiful poem of my life, one I rewrite every day...
and unknowingly, you're still the heroine in it.

8.

You once said, "I don't understand you." The truth is you never tried. I wanted you to read me like a love poem. But you were a girl of calculations,
searching for profits, not poetry.

9.

You left with the guy who brings you flowers every day. And I stayed behind, the one whose pen
blooms flowers for you every night. You never realized, Flowers can be bought...Poetry cannot.

10.

I loved you so deeply that I could've written an entire book about you. But I didn't. Because even though you know how to read, you never tried to understand.

11.
That night, when you said, We're not meant to be, I smiled and replied- "It's okay." But what you never knew is, that same night, I picked up my pen for the first time... and that was the night my journey as a poet began.

First Glance, Final Hope

1.
It all started with a "Hi" on Instagram, A soft rhythm of love echoed in my heart. Never saw you face to face,Yet my soul searched only for you, Felt like you were mine-forever, every day.

2.
That first call on New Year's Eve, Love lines drawn on clouds, in dreams I believe. My heart was heavy with a thousand thoughts,
What if we meet and you don't feel the same, That fear never left my name.

3.
You sat quietly on the park bench, Smiled and said, "You're a little different, you know?"
When our eyes met, my heart trembled, Something inside whispere"She's my whole world."

4.

I stood outside your house that day, First time I was so brave for someone I hardly knew. You sat on my bike, gently held my hand, And from that moment on, The road felt brighter, more alive than ever before.

5.

You sat behind me, learning how to ride, The wind whispered our names in love's tide. Each turn of the road told a new tale, And you,, You were the most beautiful line in the poetry of my life.

6.

I still wonder, what would've happened if you weren't there? Would love still feel this real, this rare?
Instagram, the park, the bike were all just excuses.
The truth is, You were always the address to my heart.

7.

Love kept growing, day by day, Every word carried the rhythm of your name.Then suddenly, you became silent And I knew, You now belonged to someone else's dawn.

8.

Your memories are still written in my diary, Even now, I can't find myself without you. You left-without a single word, And I didn't even ask "why", Because love doesn't mean holding back- Sometimes letting go is also love.

9.
You know, I still stare at your photo, Searching for that old "I love you" in messages. You now belong in someone else's story, And I remain in the pages of your past An old chapter, That never really ended.

10.
Your smile no longer belongs to me, Yet I still love that smile the most. Because you were my whole world, And I was just a silent spectator- Whose love ended in a one-sided curse.

11.
You said you'd stay forever, And now, I'm not even in your shadow. Maybe my love had flaws, But believe me, Chasing after you, I lost myself completely.

12.
Is love really so fragile, That it changes just by seeing someone else? You said, "I don't love you anymore."
I said, "Alright." But the sound of my breaking heart,
No one heard.

13.
I thought I'd survive even if you left, But your absence turned each breath into poison. In loving you,
I lost myself.

14.
Even now, I wake up at midnight, Thinking you messaged me again. But the screen remains silent,
And my heart slowly shatters Still full of emotions,
All tied to you.

15.
You left without a single reason, And I still search for it every day. Maybe you did the right thing, But I'm still stuck in the illusion Where love only meant 'you'.

16.
Memories don't make me cry anymore,
They just leave me wondering How did you forget so easily? Was love just a word for you? For me, it was a sacred promise.

A Love Beyond Caste

1.
"Caste" is just a name... My love was real.
But the girl I loved, She couldn't give me her name.

2.
She didn't belong to me, yet I called her mine. She never promised, yet I kept believing. She was never mine...Still, I lost everything to her.

3.
She didn't have to leave me.. Just a word, and I'd have left myself.

4.
She moved on so easily- As if I was just a story she read and forgot. But I'm still stuck in the same chapter, Unable to write "The End."

5.
She said "Don't wait for me." But she forgot
I never chose to wait, I was just unable to leave.

6.
No, I'm not angry. Just a little silent, a little broken,
And a lot more empty than you'll ever know.

7.

When love is true, You don't need promises. Just their presence is enough To keep you alive.

8.

People say love is beautiful- Maybe they've never loved someone Who was never meant to stay.

9.

I didn't lose her... I just couldn't win against her world.

10.

There was no goodbye, No last hug, no final glance...
Just silence. And that silence killed me.

11.

I didn't ask her to stay forever, Just wanted her to stay a little longer. But maybe even that was too much.

12.

You can delete pictures, Block numbers, burn letters,
But how do you erase someone from your soul?

13.

She didn't betray me... She just chose someone
Who made life easier- Not deeper.

14.

In every love story, There's always one who leaves
And one who breaks.

15.
They ask, “Why do you still love her?”
I smile and say "Some feelings don’t need reasons,
They just become prayers."

16.
I wish I had un-heard her goodbye. Maybe I would’ve kept believing, That she still cared.

17.
People change, Feelings fade, But memories?
They stay like scars.

18.
She wasn’t just a part of my life- She was my life.
And now...I’m just surviving.

19.
I loved her in silence...She left with noise. And now,
My silence is louder than ever.

20.
Even if we weren’t meant to be, I’ll still love her
The way the moon loves the night,
Distant... yet always there.

Fell in love Through the Keypad

1)
You weren't around, neither was a smartphone-
yet, there was love. Something was definitely there...
like half-written messages
still sitting in a forgotten Facebook inbox.

2)
2G internet, an old Nokia phone- and yet, staying up late at night felt real. Even more real was the wait for your simple "Hi."

3)
Your name is still in my friend list- but not in the inbox of my heart. Because that day,
you truly logged out... forever.

4)
You once said-
"Distance doesn't matter, only connection does."
And one day, you casually added-
"That guy from Delhi just gets me more..."

5)
You deleted my contact, and I never blamed you.
Even if the love got lost- that old SMS tone still soundsjust the same.

6)
The old inbox, once filled with words- I scroll through it now, where once lived love, now remains only history.

7)
Once we were 'friends', then 'lovers', and now... just 'acquaintances'. Love quietly hides its face
in the silence of the last seen message.

8)
There was a time when I feared calling you-
worried my talk time would run out. Now, I have full balance... but nothing left to say- and no one on the other side.

9)
You deleted everything... but I saved it all-
our conversations, in a notepad I titled: "Old Gold."

10)
The love wasn't a lie- the timing was. You weren't a mistake... but maybe that 'Add Friend' button
on Facebook was.

11.
I used to cherish those days,
when even a simple message brought a smile.
You were far away, yet it felt like
this distance itself was the closest kind of love.

12.
What a strange yet beautiful feeling it was,
when even a plain message held colorful dreams.
We were so easily happy back then,
our love story lived within the screen of a phone.

13.
It all began with a simple "Hi" on Facebook.
Every word exchanged felt like a blessing.
You had no idea how many times I refreshed the notification bar just to see your reply.

14.
Love back then was pure and simple, no video calls, no filters. Yet I saw my future in your pictures.
And now, even with everything available, that reality seems lost.

15.
You were 2,000 kilometers away, yet you lived so close to my heart. Love doesn't always need physical presence, sometimes, it's just about soul understanding soul.

16.
You used to say, "There's something different about you." And I believed I was lucky. But luck never stays for long, it came... and so did your goodbye.

17. Once I believed you and I were forever. Now I understand, some stories are meant to remain incomplete. Your silence became the loudest reply.
And I've learned, even silent love can be a form of farewell.

18.
Those short little texts of yours, are still etched on the walls of my heart. I haven't forgotten you,
I've just forgotten the habit of speaking with you.

19.
You walked away with someone else.
And I remained, living in old screenshots.
Strange, isn't it? I still can't bring myself to delete them, as if they're the only pictures I have of you in my heart.

20.
You were wrong when you said, "Love happens only once." You were my first, but you taught me that even the first one can end.
Now, whenever someone comes close, I get scared,
what if they vanish just like you?

21.
You don’t message me anymore. Maybe you’ve even deleted my number. But believe me,
on my phone, your name is still saved the same,
"My First Love."

22.
We were friends... then lovers... and now, just people who exist in each other’s memories. Maybe our love lost to time, but the feelings? They still remain undefeated.

23.
I still write for you. You don’t know maybe you don’t even care to. But every word carries a trace of you.
Because loving you... made me a poet.

24.
Many love with their bodies, I loved you with my soul.
Even in distance, you felt closest. Today, even in the crowd,most feel like strangers.

25.
You must be doing well now. And me?
I read your old messages... and write new stories from the ruins.

26.
Your single “Hi” used to brighten my day. Now my phone barely holds charge, but back then,
those messages used to charge my heart.

27.
You may be gone, but your story still continues in my words. Because some love stories don't need an ending to live forever.

28.
Today, I saw your profile update, "Engaged to someone." A strange smile came to my lips...
and somewhere deep inside, a quiet tear.

29.
Losing you gave me poetry. Forgetting you led me to find my voice. If you hadn't left, maybe I'd never have written so deeply. In your absence, I found my true self.

30.
You became just a story... and I, its storyteller.
I still love you, but now, it no longer hurts.
It just lingers... as a quiet feeling.

When Love Was Just a Whisper

1.

Some people don't leave you when they walk away, they stay behind in the silences, in old songs,
in memories you can't delete. Their absence becomes louder than their presence ever was, echoing in every room they never even entered.

2.

I wasn't a page in her story, just a faded line she once underlined and forgot. She smiled like I was the only one, but moved on like I was no one.
That's how love feels sometimes unfinished.

3.

She never said goodbye, just stopped answering,
like silence was enough to explain everything.
But I still talk to her in my dreams, still hold on to words she never said, still wait for a closure that will never come.

4.
When it rained that day, it wasn't the sky crying,
it was me. The clouds just covered it up.
I walked in the downpour, hiding my tears, hoping someone would understand, the weight of a heart drowning quietly.

5.
Eyes don't lie.
They speak a language the mouth forgets,
a glance can whisper a thousand unsaid words.
That day, her eyes met mine and everything we didn't sayscreamed louder than the world around us.

6.
Some goodbyes aren't loud. They don't slam doors or scream at night. They just stop calling,
stop caring,
and fade like evening light. But their silence lingers,
like a slow poison you can't stop drinking.

7.
The night she left, even the stars lost their shine.
The sky seemed dull,
like it too mourned a love story left halfway. And I... I just sat under it,
watching the emptiness grow above and within.

8.

I clung to the memories like lifelines, every laugh, every touch, every late-night call. But she let go so easily, like we were just a passing moment. I guess love hits harder when you're the only one holding on.

9.

In every crowd, I search for your eyes, not your face, not your voice,just the comfort of that one familiar glance. But I only find strangers now,
and a loneliness that feels too familiar.

10.

Love doesn't leave. People do. And when they go,
they take parts of you, the parts that smiled more, trusted more. What's left behind isn't a broken heart,
it's a version of you that no longer believes.

11.

My heart still echoes your last words, not because they were poetic, but because they were final.
Every heartbeat is a reminder of a moment when something beautiful ended, without warning, without mercy.

12.

Sometimes, it's not the person we miss, but the version of us we were with them. The laughter, the belief in forever, the joy of innocence.
Some moments are so pure, you can't help falling for them again and again.

13.
You weren't a habit, you were an addiction, a rhythm my heart danced to.
Even today, I wake up expecting your name on my phone.
Some memories don't fade, they grow stronger in your absence.

14.
I didn't write my feelings in letters, I stored them in glances, in long stares, in tears I never let fall.
Because some emotions are too fragile for words,
too raw to be spoken aloud.

15.
In front of the world, I was all smiles- loud, cheerful, okay. But behind those smiles were sleepless nights,
soaked pillows, and silent screams.
No one ever knew the clown cried after the show.

16.
Loving you was like chasing shadows, beautiful from afar, but always slipping through.
I lost myself trying to hold onto
someone who was never mine to begin with.But love doesn't ask permission, it just stays.

17.
She came into my life like a poem, soft, rhythmic, full of meaning. And one day, she left like a silent tear,
no sound, no explanation, just a sting that lingered
long after the lines were erased.

18.

Your silence didn't hurt me. What shattered me was your absence, how you stopped being a part of my days. No texts, no calls, just an empty space where love once breathed.

19.

You feel like a stranger now,
but I knew you once.
I knew your dreams, your fears,
your favorite songs.
Funny how people become strangers
when memories fade and love dies quietly.

20.

I still leave a space for you, in my poems, in my prayers,in
that one side of the bed I don't touch.
You're gone,but the place you left behind
still whispers your name every night.

Incomplete Love, Undying Words

1.
Sometimes, we walk too close to someone, only to realize. people are most beautiful when viewed from a distance. Proximity reveals scars, silence, and truth we weren't prepared to face.

2.
Make one mistake, and they will forget everything you did right. Loyalty fades in seconds when memories become selective and hearts choose convenience over compassion.

3.
Some stories end in love, and some loves remain just stories. Not every heartbeat finds a forever; some just echo endlessly in pages left unread.

4.
We often give our all to those who were never meant to stay. The ones we fight the most for, walk away without a glance.

5.
Even the strongest hearts grow tired- tired of waiting, tired of trying, tired of hoping that one day, love will feel like it once did.

6. There are people who teach you love, not by staying, but by leaving. And in their absence, you learn what your soul truly needed.
7. Sometimes, the person who once made you feel alive becomes the reason behind your silent nights and sleepless dreams.

8.
You don't always lose someone when they walk away. Sometimes, the loss began long before, when they stopped listening, stopped caring, stopped being there.

9.
We smiled through the pain, hoping love would notice. But love only watched, indifferent and silent, as we crumbled beneath expectations.

10.
The worst goodbyes are the ones left unsaid. No closure. No explanations.
Just silence that screams louder than any farewell ever could.

11.
I gave pieces of myself to someone who never looked back. Now I search for me in the ruins of a love that never truly saw me.

12.
Love doesn't always heal.
Sometimes, it teaches you how to live
broken, quietly, gently, like a flower blooming in the dark.

13.
We build forever on fragile promises.
Then watch it collapse,
wondering why temporary hearts couldn't hold eternal dreams.

14.
You can forgive a thousand times, but love dies a little with every disappointment.
Not all wounds bleed, some just turn into silence.

15.
She left with my laughter, my dreams, my peace. Now, I carry only echoes, reminders of a love that was louder than my pain.

16.
I still remember the warmth of your hands, the way your silence killed more than your words ever could.

17.
Not every love story ends in goodbye. Some just dissolve, like rain on old paper, slowly fading into unreadable memories.

18.
Love made me a poet, but heartbreak made me real. It's easy to write about joy- pain, however, teaches you truth.

19.
We weren't meant to last, but I still thank the stars for you. Because even broken memories shine under moonlight.

20. If only love came with guarantees. But hearts aren't contracts- they're fragile letters sent without return addresses, hoping to be understood.

Love Arrived by Train

1.
We were friends first, on a Facebook page,
Drawn to each other by an unknown pull, hand in hand. I searched for your name on hostel walls,
A message from you made my heart fly like a bird.

2.
You didn't have a mobile, yet somehow, You found me through someone else's phone. Love blossomed under the shade of friendship, And with just a glance, love was spoken.

3.
Every day, I passed by your house,
We exchanged quiet glances from the corners of our eyes. Seeing you brought a smile to my face, And in that smile, my mornings turned colorful.

4.
Three years passed in countless stories, I got lost in dreams, all drenched in your love. You moved to a different hostel, But my heart remained addicted to your smile.

5.
You called me for the first time to meet, I boarded the train, carrying the risk in my heart. I didn't know the station at all, But I took each step with the courage of love.

6.
I bought the ticket and sat on the train, My heart trembled with fear and excitement. I was just hoping to see you, And when I reached, it felt like I touched a dream.

7. You came to receive me silently, With shy love shining in your eyes and face. We walked alone along the park path, As if my heart's chariot moved beside yours.

8.
We took a picture sitting in the park, In your eyes, I saw silent poetry. That picture is still safely kept,
Where love continues to smile quietly.

9.
You held my hand, and I held yours,
The pages of our hearts opened to one another. We left footprints on the beach's sand, Adding new layers to our love story.

10.
The waves of the beach were playful like our smiles,
We were swings of love, swaying in joy. Holding hands, we walked a long road, And it felt like time stood still in that moment.

11.
After returning, I dropped you off at the hostel,
My heart remained in your lap.
I returned to my own destination,
But my mind stayed in that evening of our meeting.

12.
Love may have started from friendship, You realized later–I had already drowned in it alone. That childish love still lives on, Every evening smiles in your name.

13.
You called, and I came running, Hiding my fears, I fell deeply in love. I didn't know the way, yet I walked like a madman, A glimpse of you was my night's light.

14.
The journey from friend to lover wasn't easy,
But hearts know whose eyes carry love. One message from you, one phone call, Would take away my sleep and brighten my day.

15.
Our Facebook friendship brewed over cups of coffee,
Love came suddenly with the touch of your smile.
I used to show your picture and say- this is the girl,
For whom I'm willing to change my entire life.

16.
Even hostel life holds those memories, A day without your call felt so dull. When I didn't hear from you, restlessness grew, That's love-quiet, yet deeply rooted.

17.
I had asked for just one day from you, A day where only you and I would be together. You gave me that day, and I captured it in a photo, I framed it in my heart for the future.

18.
Being with you, I learned so much- To conquer fear, to touch dreams through a single touch. You weren't just love, you were courage- With that courage,
I crossed the railway lines to reach you.

19. Those three years of love, Smiles, tears, and stories of waiting were like pages of a novel.
You had said-"One day, we'll meet again,"
And I walked that path with pure faith.

20.
Even now I look at that photo, Where you stood by me, smiling fearlessly. That smile still speaks to me,
Love never grows old, it only turns silent.

21.
You had said "Love means trust," And I jumped into it, again and again. A few words from you, a small smile, Would carry me through the whole day like sunlight.

22.
That train journey was my first trip of love,
Thatticket, that route I still remember with shivers.
You weren't beside me, but always in my eyes,
Because love is being close from the heart, isn't it?

23.
Sitting beside you on the park bench,
That moment was our first sight of love.
You said nothing, yet I understood everything
Because love is weaving stories in silence.

24.
We left footprints on the beach water, Hoping they'd stay forever. The waves did erase them,
But your shadow is still written in my heart for eternity.

25.
Even after you left, I remember that railway station every day. Because from there began
The most beautiful journey of love in my life.

26.

Love was never easy, Yet I'd pay any price just to see you once. From friend to lover, and lover to memory,
That's life... a poem made with you in it.

27.

I don't know where you are now, But even today, when the phone rings, I search for your name.
I say I'll forget, but I never do, Because love isn't something you forget, It's something you live.

28.

Through the open hostel window, I used to think of you all night. I counted stars in your name,
Yet I could never express how much I loved you did you know?

29.

It was for you that I took that train alone, I had never felt that kind of courage before. If you call me again,
I'll cross any path once more- bravely, lovingly.

30.

Today I'm writing your story on this page, From Facebook friendship to beach walks. It all remains etched in my memory, Because love never truly ends,
It stays behind like a shadow.

Pages Of You

1.
I watched you fall out of love Like it was easy, like I was nothing. Now I sleep next to regrets And dream about the love, That died before it ever got the chance To live completely.

2.
You left without warning, But your absence echoes louder Than your presence ever did.
I sit in silence, Listening to the sound Of everything we could've been Crumbling inside me Like unread letters.

3.
Every word you said Still hangs in my mind
Sweet lies wrapped in love's disguise.
You left me with hope, Then stole even that. Now I'm left rewriting Our story alone In chapters of pain.

4.
I held your love like fire, It warmed me, Then burned me Without mercy. Now the ashes remain,
Scattered across memories I can't erase, Reminding me of all That almost was.

5.
You walked away so gently I didn't even notice
You were gone Until the emptiness inside Started to echo
With the sound of your silence, Louder than all
Your sweet lies.

6.
I believed in forever Until your goodbye Taught me the meaning Of temporary. Now I carry our memories
Like sharp glass In soft hands Each one cuts deeper
Than the last.

7.
You weren't just a person, You were a home I built in my heart. And now that you're gone, I'm homeless
In every emotion I try to live in.

8.
You promised you'd stay, But your promises Were lighter than the wind. Now all I have Are empty echoes And a heart That still waits
In a world you've forgotten.

9.
The hardest part Wasn't losing you, It was learning
You never truly belonged to me. Just a visitor
In my life, Leaving behind broken smiles
And haunting goodbyes.

10.
Your love was a lesson I never wanted to learn.
But now, every tear Teaches me pain, And every memory
Is a test I keep failing.

11.
You didn't just leave, You erased me From every sentence We wrote together. Now I rewrite stories
Alone, Still searching for meaning In the silence you left behind.

12.
You gave me a heart Filled with stars, Then stole the sky.
Now I'm just a constellation Of what we could have been.

13.
I still text you And delete it. Because some goodbyes
Don't happen once They happen, Every time I remember
What it felt like To be yours.

14.
You became a stranger With memories of my soul.
And I'm here, A familiar face In a story
You no longer read.

15.
Love didn't break me Your version of love did.
You taught me, That people can hold you So close And still feel So far.

16.

I keep your name In poems You'll never read. Because some feelings Are too heavy For closure, But too light To forget.

17.

Your goodbye was silent, But the silence screams louder, Than your love ever did. Now I sleep with echoes, Dreaming of you In places
You never belonged.

18.

I gave you everything, My love, my time, Even parts of me
I never showed anyone. And all I got back
Was the sound Of my heart breaking
In your absence.

19.

They say love heals, But yours left scars Even time avoids. Now I wear pain Like perfume, Lingering in every word I write About you.

20.

I waited at the end Of every chapter For you to return.
But you were always The unfinished sentence,
A story That stopped making sense When you left.

21.
You taught me How to feel alive And then killed
Every reason to. Now I'm just A graveyard of feelings
You once touched.

22.
You were the storm That made me feel, Alive and destroyed. Now I sit in calm, Missing the chaos
You used to bring With every glance.

23.
You didn't just leave, You forgot how to love me
While I was still loving you With every breath
I had left.

24.
I didn't fall in love I drowned in it.
And you, You swam away While I sunk With every memory You left behind.

25.
Your name is now A wound that smiles.
It hurts, But I can't stop saying it In my poems.

26.
Love shouldn't hurt, But with you, It became a lesson
In surviving heartbreak With a smile That lies.

27.

Even after you left, I kept setting places For your love
At the table Of my heart. Now I dine alone With ghosts.

28.

We weren't a tragedy, We were worse: A story that never had The chance to bloom Before it withered.

29.

You weren't my whole world, But you were the best part of it. Now the rest Feels like Empty space.

30.

You were poetry In motion, And I was the pause
You never read aloud. Left behind In silence, Still rhyming with heartbreak.

About The Author

Kunal Roy is a writer who believes that words have the power to heal, connect, and give voice to the unspoken emotions of the heart. Through his poetry, he captures the essence of love, longing, joy, and pain, weaving them into verses that touch the soul.

His debut book, Dil Ke Alfaaz, is a heartfelt collection that reflects not only his personal journey but also the emotions every reader can relate to. For Kunal, writing is more than expression. it is a way to reach hearts, inspire thoughts, and preserve feelings in timeless words.

With a passion for literature and a deep love for meaningful expression, Kunal aspires to continue writing and sharing his thoughts with readers, hoping that his words will always find a home in someone's heart.

Author's Note

Dear Reader,

Every word in this book is a piece of my heart, woven with emotions I could not keep within myself. Dil Ke Alfaaz is not just a collection of poems. it is a reflection of moments, feelings, and silent whispers that often go unheard in the noise of life.

If, while reading, you find even a single line that feels like it was written for you, then my purpose as a writer is fulfilled. This book is not mine alone; it belongs to every soul who has ever loved, lost, hoped, or dreamed.

Thank you for allowing me to share my words with you. May these verses stay with you long after the pages are closed.

With love and gratitude,
Kunal Roy

www.ingramcontent.com/pod-product-compliance
Lightning Source LLC
Chambersburg PA
CBHW050026170726
48282CB00025B/564
* 9 7 8 9 3 3 4 3 7 9 7 4 7 *